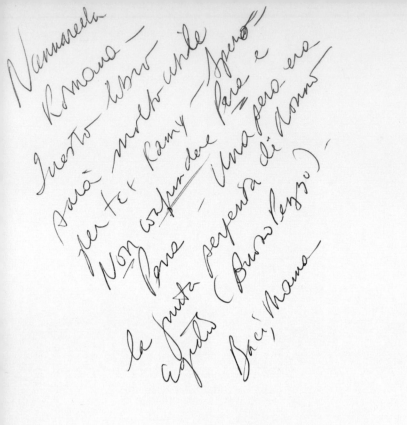

Nannarella
Romana —
Questo libro —
sarà molto utile
per te e Ramy — Spero —
Non so per dove Parte, e
Pane — Una pera era
la punta perfetta di Roma
a quella (Buon Pezzo)
Baci, Mama

Natale 1995
Lyme, NH USA

# PEARS

A COUNTRY GARDEN COOKBOOK

# PEARS

## A COUNTRY GARDEN COOKBOOK

*By Janet Hazen*

*Photography by Kathryn Kleinman*

CollinsPublishersSanFrancisco

*A Division of HarperCollinsPublishers*

*First published in USA 1994 by Collins Publishers San Francisco*
*Copyright © 1994 by Collins Publishers San Francisco*
*Recipe and text copyright © 1994 Janet Hazen*
*Photographs copyright © 1994 Kathryn Kleinman*
*Food Stylist: Stephanie Greenleigh*
*Floral and Prop Stylist: Michaele Thunen*
*Creative Director: Jennifer Barry*
*Designer: Kari Perin*
*Series Editor: Meesha Halm*
*The pear branch illustration on page 35 is from* The Best of the Old Farmer's
Almanac *by Will Forpe. Copyright © 1977 by Jonathan David Publishers.*
*Photograph on page 2 by Elizabeth Zeschin.*
*Library of Congress Cataloging-in-Publication Data*
*Hazen, Janet.*
*Pears: a country garden cookbook/by Janet Hazen;*
*photography by Kathryn Kleinman.*
*p. cm.*
*Includes index.*
*ISBN 0-00-255345-7*
*1. Cookery (Pears) I. Title.*
*TX813.P43H39 1994*
*641.6'413—dc20 CIP 94-2111*
*All rights reserved, including the right of reproduction in whole*
*or in part or in any form.*
*Printed in China*
*1 3 5 7 9 10 8 6 4 2*

### Acknowledgments

*Collins and the photography team would like to thank*
*Terry Greene, photo assistant; Cachet Bean, production assistant;*
*Laura Jerrard, food styling assistant; Kristen Wurz, design*
*and production coordinator; and Jonathan Mills, production manager.*
*Thanks also to Ray Bair; Ken Poisson and Yvette Poisson;*
*Pam and Ron Kaiser from Westside Farms in Healdsburg; and*
*Martine Gauthier from Savoir Vivre in San Francisco.*

# CONTENTS

# INTRODUCTION

Few fruits conjure a more clear and distinct image than the pear. With its graceful, voluptuous contour, it is easily one of the most provocative and sensuous fruits in the world.

Knowing that a new crop of pears is right around the corner makes the fading of summer and its glorious bounty a bearable passing. By late September, ruby-violet berry stains are replaced by clear, fragrant pear juice. Unlike showy flamboyant summer fruits that shout summer, pears, in their understated, refined and subtle fashion, discreetly suggest autumn. Mirroring the colors of the season, they arrive with cloaks colored saffron yellow and burnt orange, rusty red and crimson, toasty brown and cinnamon. They beg for cool-weather flavor companions such as hazelnuts and pecans, brown butter and caramel, cinnamon and nutmeg. Their handsome colors and velvety texture inspire thoughts of cooking, baking, poaching and otherwise turning these delightful fruits into tempting edibles.

The pear is one of the most ancient of cultivated fruits. Originally grown in the area around the Caucasus Mountains between Russia and Turkey, the pear was spread by Aryan tribes as they migrated into Europe and northern India. Pears are of the *Pyrus* genus and are closely related to apples and quinces. The European varieties come from *P. communis* and *P. nivalis*. The Asian varieties, often called apple-pears, come from *P. pyrifolia* and *P. ussuriensis*. While the geographic development of Asian varieties occurred separately from the European, their parallel history makes them kindred fruits.

Traces of pears are evident as far back as ten thousand years ago in Ice Age dwellings found in Switzerland. One of the earliest written records of the fruit was made by Sumerian secretaries around 2750 B.C. In the text they describe a thick paste made from pears, thyme and figs mixed with oil and ale to be made into a poultice and applied to the body.

The ancient Greeks held the pear in high esteem; Homer called the fruit "the gift of the gods." In the fourth century B.C., the Greek naturalist Theophrastus, a student of Aristotle, wrote detailed information about the propagation of pears. Along with grapes and apples, pears were also a common fruit of imperial Rome. Records show that the Romans developed, or at least discovered, approximately 38 pear varieties and in turn introduced them to the nations of their vast empire. During this time pears were customarily enjoyed after a meal, although some were pickled or preserved by submerging them whole in vessels of honey.

Chinese documentation of pears dates back to 1000 B.C. In the third century A.D., the writer Ko Nigung outlined the various Chinese pear varieties available, and in sixth century writings there are descriptions of the different propagation techniques employed.

By the Middle Ages, pear cultivation in Europe was confined primarily to castle and monastery gardens, thus making pears a luxury item available to a select group. This aristocratic image was still associated with the fruit in the seventeenth century, when pear growing in private orchards became a hobby for the wealthy. In France during this time, pear growing reached its zenith when numerous new varieties were developed. In the eighteenth century, the Belgians were the leading innovators. It was a Belgian, Nicolas Hardenpont, who stole the limelight in the eighteenth century with the first butter pear varieties. Soft, ultrajuicy and flavorful, these pears were a vast improvement over existing varieties.

The early colonial settlers introduced the pear to North America around 1629. Most of the European pear varieties grown in North America are over one hundred years old, and of the thousands of registered varieties, none are indigenous to the continent. The major commercially grown pears in the United States are all descendants of European varieties or are hybrids created by crossing European with Asian strains.

Today over 5,000 varieties of domestic pears are grown throughout the world's temperate zones. The major commercial growing areas for both European and Asian pear varieties in the United States are California, Oregon and Washington. France, which has long had a reputation for growing superior pears, is now the European leader in their cultivation.

Although the appearance of pears in the markets traditionally signals the arrival of autumn, contemporary packing and shipping procedures now enable us to have a year-round supply of the fresh fruit.

Because pears are one of the few fruits that actually ripen more successfully off the tree, they are picked when green and hard. (When left on the tree to ripen, the fruit becomes soft at the core and mealy.) This is a boon for growers, who can transport their crops with minimum damage. It also means that once purchased, you must allow pears time to ripen at home, a process that requires diligent monitoring, since pears move from a state of perfect ripeness to unpleasant spoilage with surprising speed.

Although people are most familiar with the greenish yellow–skinned Bartlett or Packham varieties that are ubiquitous in supermarkets, there is actually much diversity in pear color and size. From the brownish gold Bosc to the fiery Red Crimson, and from the amply proportioned yellow Anjou to the diminutive Seckel, each variety has a unique flavor, texture, color and size. Although I have suggested commonly available varieties for each of the recipes in this book, I encourage you to use some of the lesser-known pears also mentioned.

In many of these recipes I have used various components of ethnic cuisines as inspiration for developing new dishes, while in others I have re-created classics to satisfy traditionalists who crave something comforting and familiar. The mild flavor and buttery texture of the versatile pear allow it to shine in everything from delicate green salads and spicy chutneys to earthy pasta dishes and decadent desserts. I hope you will use these recipes to find new ways to enjoy the perfumed and delicate, lightly sweet flavor of this most sensuous fruit.

# GLOSSARY

**Selecting:** When selecting European pear varieties, look for relatively smooth, unblemished skin devoid of dents, holes, marks or bruises. The fruit ought to feel firm to the touch, as it will probably be underripe.

In contrast to the European varieties, Asian pears are sold in a near ripe or fully ripe condition. They ought to be hard to the touch with crisp flesh, even when ripe. To determine the ripeness of a brown-skinned Asian pear, look for fruit with an overall, even-colored skin tone with very few, if any, medium-green or medium-tawny patches. A ripe yellow-skinned Asian pear will be uniformly colored and devoid of pale green or whitish yellow spots. Avoid buying Asian pears that are soft or mushy in any way.

If you're fortunate, your produce market or grocery store offers a wide selection of pears from which to choose. Asian pears may not be as readily available as European varieties. Search for these pears in natural food stores, specialty produce shops and Asian food markets. Your favorite produce vendor may be able to special order them for you.

The recipes in this book call for a range of fairly common European pears. If you can't find one of the suggested types, choose a comparable variety in the same size range. European and Asian pears, however, are not truly interchangeable, so it's best to use one of the varieties specified in each recipe. If you are intent on preparing a dish that calls for Asian pears and you simply cannot find them, you may substitute a slightly underripe Bosc or Winter Nelis pear.

Most recipes that utilize pears in their uncooked state call for fully ripened fruit. When selecting pears to use in any of these recipes, consider the variety, size, shape, skin and flesh color, texture, flavor and ripeness. When a recipe calls for a "firm-but-ripe" pear, choose a ripe European variety that, even when ripe, has a fairly firm texture; Bosc, Winter Nelis and Seckel pears fit this description. Used alone, the word "firm" in the recipes refers to pears that are flavorful but slightly underripe (firm in texture). When it calls for "ripe" pears, the fruit must be at their prime—tender, juicy and fragrant, with fully developed flavor.

**Storing:** It's best to store underripe European pears at room temperature, allowing them to ripen naturally. Ripening time varies depending upon the size, type and level of maturity when purchased, but most fruit will be ready to eat within two to four days if ripened at a cool room temperature. You may retard the ripening process by loosely wrapping the fruit in butcher or wax paper and storing them in the refrigerator. Conversely, you may hasten the ripening process by placing the pears in a tightly sealed brown paper bag, alone or with a piece of ripe stone fruit (such as a plum, nectarine or peach), at room temperature for one to two days or until the fruit is ripe.

Store Asian pears in a tightly sealed plastic bag in the refrigerator until ready to use. Most Asian pears, depending on their size and maturity when purchased, will keep in the refrigerator for up to two weeks.

**Eating:** Since most of us judge the ripeness of fruit by how it feels in our hand (the softer the feel, the more juicy and flavorful the flesh), it may take a while to adjust our "ripeness barometer" to accurately rate pears. A European pear is ready to eat when it yields slightly to gentle pressure next to the stem and its sweet perfume fills the air. If a pear is soft and mushy on the exterior, you can count on the interior being unpleasantly mealy, dry and tasteless.

Although Asian pears are usually sold nearly ripe, for optimal flavor, wait for the skin to turn a uniform color before eating, but do so before the fruit becomes soft to the touch.

**Preparing:** To remove the skin from a pear, hold the fruit firmly in one hand and, using a sharp paring knife, carefully remove the thin outer layer of skin. You can also use a sharp vegetable peeler to remove the skin, but if the blades are not extremely sharp, or if the pear is very ripe and on the soft side, you could wind up with a handful of crushed fruit, skin and juice running down the length of your arm!

To core a whole pear, place the fruit on a flat surface with the stem up. Holding a sharp apple or pear corer (a practical tool sold in specialty cookware shops or the culinary section of department stores) by the handle, place the round, open end directly over the stem on top of the pear. Firmly yet carefully, press the corer straight down through the center and out the bottom of the pear. Remove the corer by lifting it, and the core and seeds contained within, straight up and out through the top of the pear. Remove any seeds remaining in the cavity using a narrow implement.

Although it is a bit clumsy and the results are less tidy in appearance, you can also core a pear using a small, narrow paring knife. Enter through the bottom of the pear, carefully cutting the core and seeds from the center, and take care not to remove too much of the edible flesh. In this instance, you don't need to cut all the way through the top of the pear.

To halve and core a pear, firmly hold the pear on its side on a cutting board. Using a sharp chef's knife, slice the pear in half from stem end to the bottom. Using a small paring knife, or even a small spoon if the flesh is particularly soft, remove the core and seeds from the center of each half.

To quarter a pear or cut it into long sections, first remove the stem and skin (if necessary), and firmly hold the pear on its side on a cutting board. Using a sharp chef's knife, cut the pear in half from stem to bottom. Proceed cutting into the desired number of sections and remove the core and seeds.

When a recipe calls for "pear rounds," slice the fruit across the circumference, rather than from stem end to bottom. Once sliced, you can remove the core and seeds using a small, sharp paring knife. Alternatively, you can core the pear first and then slice it into rounds. A whole, cored, very ripe, and therefore soft, pear is structurally less stable than one fully intact; when slicing an extremely ripe pear into rounds, you may want to slice it first and then remove the core and seeds from each individual slice.

Once cut and exposed to air, most pears will darken if not quickly combined with other ingredients that coat the flesh or unless they are treated with acidulated water. None of the recipes in this book use pears in such a way as to incur this problem, but should you decide to serve a few sliced pears along with some cheese and nuts, proceed with the following instructions to prevent browning: Make a solution of approximately five parts cold water to one part lemon juice (1 cup of water mixed with 3 tablespoons of lemon or lime juice is usually enough for 6 pears). Cut the pears just before serving, and lightly brush with the acidulated water. For sizable quantities, place the appropriate amount of acidulated water in a large bowl, add the pears and gently toss, coating all surfaces. Using your hands, remove the pears from the liquid and drain thoroughly in a colander. Pat dry using a clean kitchen towel if the pears are still damp.

**Cooking:** Whether blanched, braised, boiled, broiled, simmered, stewed, sautéed, fried, baked or roasted, one must take into consideration many factors when cooking with fresh pears. The constitution of a pear and its impact on a given recipe is contingent on several elements: the type of pear (European or Asian); the variety (Bosc, Forelle, Packham or French Butter, for example); the inherent texture versus its level of maturity; and the size.

Generally speaking, firm, slightly underripe European pears are preferable for cooking and baking. Asian pears, with their unusually high moisture content and naturally hard flesh, retain their shape and texture when exposed to heat and/or long periods of cooking. These attributes make Asian pears the ideal fruit to use in slow-cooked dishes where the

shape of the fruit must be preserved. Conversely, dishes that benefit from fruit that breaks down with extended cooking or high heat are best made with the more delicate, creamy-fleshed European types.

It's important to consider the moisture content when preparing baked goods that call for uncooked pears; utilizing particularly juicy, ripe fruit could result in heavy, leaden cakes, muffins, quick breads, pies or tarts. For this reason, most of my baked desserts call for slightly underripe pears. The moisture content of a pear is less critical in dishes that employ a moist-heat cooking method, such as poaching, simmering, sautéing or stewing, and in recipes where the fruit is served along with its cooking liquid. Ripe and/or naturally juicy or soft pears are good for these types of dishes.

Although we don't want the pears in any dish to be hard and dry, we also don't want mushy, mealy fruit. In most cases, if the pears are soft and grainy to begin with, cooking will only accentuate these undesirable qualities. One exception is syrup-cooked pears, where the sugar-saturated cooking liquid helps strengthen the cell walls by creating a new one comprised of sugar. Pears cooked in this manner not only taste good, but the high concentration of sugar also restores texture to the fruit by drawing some of the water back into the flesh.

**Note:** The availability of pear varieties listed in this glossary may vary from region to region and may shift slightly due to unexpected changes in climate, growing conditions, diseases and other natural occurrences.

**European Pears:**

*Anjou:* Available October through January. Often marketed as d'Anjou, named after the Anjou region of France especially known for its pears. Large, thin-skinned yellowish green pear with a subtle, graceful shape. Texture ranges from medium-grain to coarse, depending on ripeness. Flesh can range from juicy to mealy with a mild and delicate, concentrated flavor. When slightly underripe, the Anjou is excellent for cooking and baking, but once it reaches maturity, save this pear for eating out of hand or using uncooked in salads.

*Bartlett:* Available July through early November. Large, bell-shaped fruit with light greenish yellow skin sometimes blushed with pale red. Decidedly sweet and herbaceous in flavor, the Bartlett's juicy, succulent flesh and fine texture make it one of the most popular eating pears in the United States. When underripe, the Bartlett is a good choice for baked goods and quick cooking stove-top dishes. Its unmistakable fragrance and definitive pear flavor make it ideal for use in both leafy green and fruit salads.

*Bosc:* Available late August through March; year-round in some areas. Medium to large pear with distinctive russet-gold skin and slender form. It has firm-textured, medium-grain, crisp, dense flesh with a unique nutty flavor that hints of vanilla, caramel, brown butter and spice. When ripe, it is juicy yet firm, making it ideal for cooking and baking.

*Comice:* Available August through November. When underripe, this medium to large pear is predominantly green; when ripe, the fruit has a medium-yellow tone with areas of light green. Mild in flavor and not too sweet, this fine-textured pear is good for use in leafy green and fruit salads, and when underripe, for cooking and baking.

*Forelle:* Available early October through February. Small to medium pear with yellow skin blushed with freckles or patches of vivid red when fully ripe. Pleasingly juicy and sweet at its prime, the Forelle pear can be unusually dry and tart when underripe. The Forelle is excellent for eating out of hand, pairing with cheese or for using in leafy green or fruit salads.

*French or Italian Butter:* Available late July through early October. Thin-skinned and small to medium in size, both the French and Italian Butter pears are very sweet and mild in flavor. Their fine-grained, ultrajuicy, pale white flesh and greenish yellow to light-rust skin make them suitable for using in recipes that call for unpeeled pears and for eating out of hand.

*Packham:* Available July through October. Occasionally referred to as Bartlett Packham, this large pear sports a light-green skin when underripe, but once fully ripened, has a distinct yellow hue. Fine-grained, moderately juicy and almost carrot-like in flavor, the Packham is excellent for cooking and baking.

*Red Anjou:* Available October through January. Medium-sized, slightly rounded pear with reddish tawny skin and areas of dusty green. The Red Anjou is firm textured, slightly dry and sometimes mealy, with subtle flavors that hint of nuts and spice. Unusual skin tone and moderate size make this pear a

Anjou

Bartlett

Bosc

Comice

Forelle

French Butter

Packham

Red Anjou

Red Bartlett

Red Blush

Red Crimson

Seckel

Winter Nelis

good contender for a wide range of cooking purposes. When underripe, it is excellent for using in chutneys or other long-cooking dishes and for baking. When perfectly ripe and in season, use uncooked in salads and desserts.

*Red Bartlett:* Available late August through late November. The Red Bartlett is a bit smaller than the greenish yellow variety, but it has a similar texture and flavor. Use this red-skinned, juicy pear in salads where a color accent is needed and in baked goods.

*Red Blush:* Available late August through February. A medium-sized pear with distinctive deep red, medium-thick skin. The sweet, juicy flesh has a slightly grainy texture that, when underripe, makes it ideal for use in baked goods and for cooking.

*Red Crimson:* Available mid-July through October. Medium- to large-sized pear with velvety, deep red skin and creamy, fine-grained white flesh. It has a juicy and buttery texture with sweet floral undertones. Excellent for eating raw or for use in cooking or baking. Rich skin tone adds depth and color to foods.

*Seckel:* Available late August through February. Comparatively thick-skinned, this tiny pear has a medium-green to russet exterior and a very pale, yellow-white interior. The juicy, fine-grained flesh is sweet, spicy and flavorful, and its firm texture (especially when slightly underripe) makes it ideal for using whole or halved in poached dishes and for canning, preserving or pickling.

*Summer Gold:* Available late June and July. Predominantly grown in Oregon, this small, squat pear has thin, pale green skin and rusty gold patches. Fairly firm in texture, the flesh is fine-grained and juicy with a bright, sometimes tart flavor with undertones of raspberry and citrus. When ripe, use the Summer Gold pear in leafy green or fruit salads and desserts; underripe it is good for cooking and baking.

*Winter Nelis:* Available late September through March. This large, round, plump European pear bears a close resemblance to the Asian varieties. Its matte, medium-brown skin makes it less suitable for using in green or fruit salads, but once peeled, the flavorful, juicy, yet firm, flesh lends itself to baked goods and savory dishes.

**Asian Pears:**

Asian pears, frequently referred to as apple-pears, bear close resemblance to large apples. Generally round and fat in shape, their skin color ranges from pale yellow to a deeper, more pronounced shade of yellow, to a dark, nutty brown.

*Chojuro:* Available late August through December. This small- to medium-sized pear has a golden brown, tawny skin and crunchy white flesh. Sweet and crisp, the Chojuro is proportioned perfectly for snacking, but it also works well in savory dishes and in leafy green and fruit salads.

*Hosui:* Available late August through January. Small to medium in size, this pear ranges from deep yellow-gold when semiripe, to a warm, toasty brown color when fully ripe. The texture is less crisp than most other Asian pears, but

Hosui

Niitaka

Shinko

Shinseiki

Twentieth Century

Ya Li

in comparison to European varieties, it is considered crisp and very juicy. The deeply flavored flesh hints of brown butter and butterscotch, making it ideal to use in desserts, salads and for eating out of hand.

*Niitaka:* Available late August through October. Small to medium in size, this round, symmetrical pear has deep yellowish brown skin and juicy flesh. Less sweet than other Asian pear varieties, the toasty, nutty, somewhat buttery-tasting qualities of the Niitaka make it perfect for use in salads and savory dishes.

*Shinko:* Available August through January. Medium to medium-large in size, this pear has a greenish undertone when underripe. When ripe, it has a rusty gold exterior and a crunchy white flesh. Ultracrisp and very juicy, the not-too-sweet flesh has an almost apple-like flavor with tart undertones. Excellent for use in savory baked and cooked dishes.

*Shinseiki:* Available late August through January. This medium-large pear has pale- to medium-yellow skin with tiny brown dots and slight mottling around the stem. Moderately crisp and juicy, the flesh has a balanced, sweet and herbaceous flavor, making it well suited for use in savory cooked or baked dishes.

*Twentieth Century or Nijisseiki:* Available late August through January. This Japanese pear is the most popular Asian pear variety both in Japan and the United States. Large, round and medium-yellow on the outside, it has a crisp, juicy flesh with sweet, nutty overtones.

*Ya Li:* Available late August through October. More elongated than the typical round Asian pear, this medium-sized unusual variety has yellow skin when perfectly ripe and a sweet, juicy flesh. Use in leafy green and fruit salads, in baked goods and in savory dishes.

*Yoinashi:* Available late August through January. Large and round, when underripe this pear has yellowish green skin that turns a lovely deep russet-gold when mature. A bit softer than other Asian pears, the flesh is still quite crisp and juicy; the flavor is mellow and sweet with honey overtones.

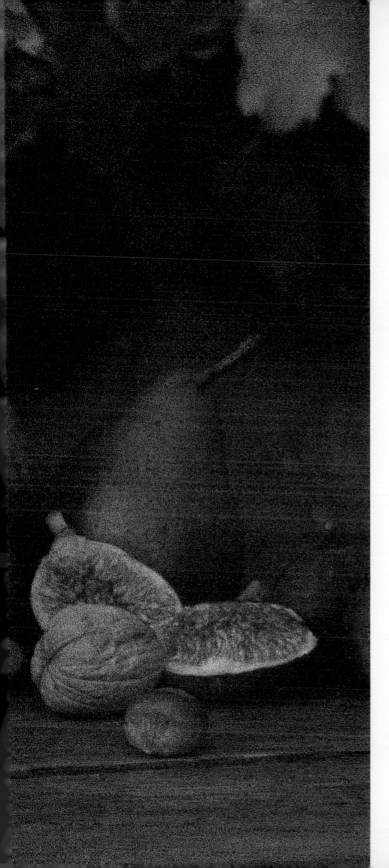

# OPENERS

There are myriad ways to use pears in hors d'oeuvres or appetizers and many good reasons for doing so. Pears are one of the most versatile fruits in the world, and their mildly sweet, subtle flavor and light texture make them ideal for starters that whet the appetite without overwhelming it.

When combined with savory ingredients, both European and Asian pears add a sweet, unexpected undertone to dishes that is very appealing. In the recipes that follow, pears are used in a variety of ways. Pairing their delicate flavor and texture with more assertively flavored ingredients is one way. Nuts, especially when roasted, accent the winning qualities of pears. Another match made in heaven is pears and cheese, as illustrated in Herbed Pear and Goat Cheese Phyllo Triangles.

Asian pears, intensely crisp and clean tasting, are perfect sliced into rounds and spread with savory toppings. The tart, almost citrus-like flavor of these distinctive pears provides a stimulating contrast to sharply flavored smoked fish, as exemplified in the recipe for Asian Pear Rounds with Smoked Salmon Cream Cheese.

A single slice of an aromatic ripe pear accompanied by a wedge of fine Stilton makes an elegant and simple appetizer. But if you're in the mood for something more creative, the recipes that follow are nearly as simple to make, and even more delicious.

# Chilled Lime-Scented Pear Soup

*The delicate essence of pears, accented by a whisper of fresh lime juice,*
*is unmistakable in this silky smooth soup. For a refreshing hot-weather lunch, serve the soup*
*in chilled bowls accompanied by a mixed green salad and bread sticks.*

*1 cup dry white wine*
*1 cup dry vermouth*
*1 cup apple-pear juice*
*5 small ripe pears (preferably Summer Gold or*
*    Italian or French Butter), peeled, cored and*
*    coarsely chopped*

*1 teaspoon ground green peppercorns**
*1/4 teaspoon ground allspice**
*Finely minced zest from 1 lime, plus additional zest,*
*    for garnish*
*Pinch of salt*
*1/4 cup fresh lime juice*

In a large, heavy-bottomed saucepan, place the wine, vermouth, apple-pear juice, pears, spices and lime zest. Bring to a boil over high heat, stirring frequently. Reduce the heat to medium and cook 10 minutes, or until the pears are tender. Remove from the heat and let cool to room temperature.

Using a blender, purée the mixture in batches until smooth. Add the salt and lime juice and mix well. Transfer to a nonreactive container and cover tightly. Refrigerate until thoroughly chilled. Serve in chilled bowls, garnished with lime zest. *Serves 4 to 6*

*Note:* Here, and throughout the book, where I call for ground spices not commonly available in this form, use an electric spice or coffee grinder to pulverize the spices.

## Broiled Asian Pears with Peppered Stilton

*In this simple recipe, crisp Asian pear rounds provide a striking contrast in
texture and flavor for barely melted English Stilton, one of the finest blue cheeses in the world.
If you can't find Stilton, any mild, semifirm blue cheese can be substituted.*

*1/2 pound Stilton cheese (rind removed), crumbled
1/2 teaspoon coarsely ground black pepper*

*2 large Asian pears (preferably Twentieth Century
or Shinseiki), cut into 1/2-inch-thick rounds,
seeds removed (approximately 8 to 10 slices)*

Preheat the broiler.

In a small bowl, combine the cheese and pepper. Using a clean kitchen towel, pat the pear slices dry and arrange in a single layer on a baking sheet.

Evenly distribute the cheese among the pear slices. Leaving a 1/2-inch border around the edge, gently flatten the cheese onto each pear slice, making an even layer.

Place under the broiler and heat until the cheese is just melted, approximately 3 minutes. Remove from the oven and serve immediately.
*Serves 4 to 6*

# Chicken Liver and Pear Spread with Hazelnuts

*The winning combination of hazelnuts and pears makes this*
*a unique chicken liver spread. This recipe is best if made a day ahead, and*
*it improves with age for up to five days in the refrigerator.*

1/3 cup hazelnuts
3 shallots, finely chopped
3 cloves garlic, minced
2 teaspoons ground coriander
1/2 teaspoon ground allspice
1/2 teaspoon ground cinnamon
1/2 teaspoon ground mace
3 tablespoons mild-flavored olive oil
3/4 cup pear eau-de-vie (such as Poire William)★

1 pound chicken livers, coarsely chopped
1 1/2 tablespoons Three-Peppercorn Pear Vinegar
   (see p. 51) or sherry vinegar
2 large firm pears (preferably Bosc, Anjou or Winter
   Nelis), peeled, cored and finely chopped
Salt and freshly ground black pepper, to taste
Crackers, croutons or thinly sliced dark rye or
   pumpernickel bread squares

Preheat the oven to 350 degrees F.

To remove the papery brown skins from the hazelnuts, arrange in a single layer on a baking sheet, place in the middle of the oven and bake 7 to 12 minutes, or until the skins turn almost black and begin to flake. Let cool to room temperature. Wrap the nuts in a clean kitchen towel and rub vigorously to remove as much of the skins as possible. Finely chop and set aside.

In a large sauté pan, cook the shallots, garlic and spices in the oil over medium heat 5 minutes, stirring frequently. Add 1/2 cup of the eau-de-vie and the chicken livers and cook over high heat approximately 3 minutes, stir-ring frequently, until the livers are just cooked. Remove from the heat and let cool slightly.

Transfer the mixture to a food processor fitted with a metal blade and add the remaining 1/4 cup eau-de-vie and the vinegar. Process until smooth. Transfer to a large bowl and add the pears and hazelnuts; mix gently. Season with salt and pepper.

Serve in an attractive bowl along with a knife for spreading onto crackers, croutons or thinly sliced dark rye or pumpernickel bread squares. *Serves 6 to 8*

★*Note:* Here, and throughout the book, where I call for pear eau-de-vie, Calvados can be substituted.

# Herbed Pear and Goat Cheese Phyllo Triangles

*Crisp Asian pears lend a pleasing texture and subtle flavor to this Greek-inspired hors d'oeuvre.*
*Choose a mild imported chèvre, such as Bucheron or Montrachet, or a young, soft domestic goat cheese.*

3/4 cup pistachios
2 medium Asian pears (preferably Chojuro or
    Hosui), halved, cored and finely chopped
3 tablespoons pear eau-de-vie (such as Poire William)
1/2 pound creamy goat cheese, softened
1/4 pound natural cream cheese, softened
1 1/2 tablespoons finely chopped fresh thyme
1 1/2 tablespoons finely chopped fresh basil

1 1/2 tablespoons finely chopped fresh parsley
1 1/2 tablespoons finely chopped fresh chives
2 teaspoons finely chopped fresh marjoram
Salt and freshly ground black pepper, to taste
1 pound phyllo dough
16 tablespoons (1/2 pound) unsalted butter, melted
1 1/2 cups finely ground almonds

Preheat the oven to 350 degrees F.

Arrange pistachios in a single layer on a baking sheet. Place in the middle of the oven and bake 10 minutes, or until nuts are light golden brown and aromatic. Let cool, then finely chop.

In a large sauté pan, cook the pears in the eau-de-vie over medium-high heat 5 minutes, stirring frequently, until the liquid has evaporated and the pears are crisp-tender. Remove from the heat; let cool to room temperature.

Place the pears in a large bowl and add the goat cheese, cream cheese, herbs and pistachios; mix well. Season with salt and pepper. Cover tightly and refrigerate until filling is thoroughly chilled, approximately 2 hours.

Lightly grease 2 baking sheets.

Lay 1 sheet of the phyllo dough out vertically on a flat surface. Keep the remaining sheets covered with a damp towel as you work. Using a pastry brush, lightly brush the entire surface of the single sheet of phyllo with melted butter. Sprinkle the buttered surface with approximately 1 tablespoon of the finely ground almonds. Cover with a second sheet and lightly brush it with butter; sprinkle with another tablespoon of almonds and cover with a third sheet of phyllo. Lightly brush the third sheet with melted butter.

Using a sharp knife and taking care not to tear the dough as you cut, divide the layered phyllo dough lengthwise into 4 equal strips. Place 1 scant tablespoon of the pear–goat cheese filling on the bottom right-hand corner of each strip. Keeping the mixture in place with your fingers, fold upward and over to make a triangle shape. Continue folding as you would a flag, making a tight, secure triangle. Fold the remaining 3 strips into triangles, brush with melted butter and place on a prepared baking sheet, leaving approximately three quarters of an inch between each triangle. Repeat with the remaining phyllo and filling.

Bake in a 350 degrees F. oven 15 to 17 minutes, or until the phyllo dough is light golden brown. Remove from the oven and serve immediately. *Serves 8 to 10*

## Grilled Pears with Prosciutto

*These neat little savory-sweet packets
are also nice served atop lightly dressed greens.*

*36 thin slices of prosciutto (approximately
    3/4 pound)
3 large ripe pears (preferably Anjou, Comice or
    Red Blush), stemmed, cut into sixths and cored
1/2 cup fruity olive oil
Freshly ground black pepper, to taste
Rosemary or oregano sprigs, for garnish*

Prepare a charcoal grill.

Using two slices for each fruit wedge, tightly wrap the prosciutto around the pears, taking care to completely cover the fruit. Brush lightly on all sides with some of the olive oil.

When the coals are medium-hot (the coals will be covered with a thin layer of gray ash), place the prosciutto-wrapped pears on the grill and cook approximately 1 to 2 minutes on the first side, or until the prosciutto turns a light brown. Carefully flip the packages and cook on the second side 2 to 3 minutes, or until the prosciutto is lightly browned and the pears are tender. Remove from the grill and sprinkle with black pepper. Serve immediately garnished with the herb sprigs. *Serves 6 to 8*

## Asian Pear Rounds with Smoked Salmon Cream Cheese

*Thickly sliced Asian pears form an ideal
base for elegant swirls of smoked salmon cream cheese
in this easy-to-prepare hors d'oeuvre.*

*1/2 pound natural cream cheese, softened to
    room temperature
1/4 pound smoked salmon, finely minced
1/3 cup finely minced fresh chives
1 tablespoon finely minced fresh parsley
2 teaspoons finely minced lemon zest
Freshly ground white pepper, to taste
3 medium Asian pears (preferably Shinseiki or
    Shinko), cored whole and sliced into 1/4-inch-
    thick rounds (approximately 20 to 21 slices)*

In a medium bowl, place the cream cheese, smoked salmon, 2 tablespoons of the chives, parsley, lemon zest and pepper. Using a hand-held electric mixer, beat 2 to 3 minutes, or until thoroughly mixed and creamy.

Place the mixture in a medium-sized pastry bag fitted with a #21 or #22 star-burst tip.

Arrange the pear slices on a large serving platter. Using a paper towel, pat dry the surface of each pear. Following the circular shape of the pear, pipe a small ribbon of the cheese mixture on top of each pear slice. Sprinkle with the remaining chives and serve immediately. *Serves 4 to 6*

# Sausage and Pear Wontons

*The combination of uncooked European and lightly cooked Asian pears adds*
*a pleasing texture and sweet undertone to the spicy sausage filling in these cross-cultural wontons.*

2 shallots, finely chopped

2 small Asian pears (preferably Chojuro, Niitaka or
    Hosui), halved, cored and finely chopped

1 tablespoon mild-flavored olive oil

1/2 pound mild Italian sausage, removed from
    the casings and finely crumbled

1 1/2 teaspoons ground fennel seeds

1 firm-but-ripe pear (preferably Packham, Bartlett or
    Winter Nelis), halved, cored and finely chopped

2 jalapeño chilies, stemmed, seeded and minced

1 clove garlic, minced

1/2 cup tomato paste

Salt and freshly ground black pepper, to taste

1/2 cup cold water

1/3 cup cornstarch

60 wonton skins (available in some produce sections
    and all Asian markets)

4 to 5 cups vegetable oil, for frying

To make the filling, in a large sauté pan, cook the shallots and Asian pears in the olive oil over high heat 2 minutes, stirring frequently. Add the sausage and fennel seeds and cook 1 1/2 minutes, stirring frequently. Remove from the heat and add the remaining pear, jalapeño, garlic and tomato paste; mix well. Season with salt and pepper. Let cool to room temperature.

In a small bowl, combine the water and cornstarch to form a slurry.

Arrange 6 to 8 wonton skins on a clean, dry, flat surface. Using a pastry brush, brush each wonton skin with a thin layer of the slurry. Immediately place approximately 1 teaspoon of the filling at one corner of each skin. Loosely fold over to make a triangle shape. Gently press each skin together starting from the inside and working toward the outside edges, expelling any air as you go. Bring the two long corners of the triangle together and

pinch together using a little slurry. Make the remaining wontons in this fashion.

Preheat the oven to 250 degrees F.

Place 2 cups of the vegetable oil in a heavy-bottomed, 6-quart pot (the oil should fill approximately one-third of the pot). Heat over medium-high heat until hot but not smoking (approximately 350 to 375 degrees F.). Add a small batch of wontons and cook 30 to 45 seconds, or until the skins are golden brown. Remove with a slotted spoon and drain on paper towels. Transfer to an oven-proof plate and keep warm in the oven. Cook the remaining wontons in small batches, adding more oil as needed. (After adding new oil to the pot, wait until it returns to the proper temperature before adding the next batch of wontons.) Serve the wontons hot. *Makes approximately 55 wontons; serves 8 to 10*

# ACCOMPANIMENTS

The recipes that follow offer a number of inviting and unexpected ways to include pears as an element in any meal. Pears have been favored as a salad ingredient for centuries. A perfectly ripe pear can elevate a common plate of greens to an unforgettable meal. When coupled with more assertive ingredients, such as smoked fish, bacon and nuts, the pear, with its sweet, juicy and tart properties, provides a lively balance. The Smoked Trout Salad with Celery and Pears, Mixed Greens with Pears and Hazelnuts, and Warm Green Salad with Pears and Bacon illustrate this affinity.

Pears have also been a popular base for chutneys and compotes. When cooked properly, they can hold their shape even through relatively long periods of cooking. This attribute, along with their adaptable flavor, makes them ideal for unhurried stove-top cooking, which allows ample time for the pears to absorb inviting spices and other flavoring agents. The Fiery East Indian Pear Chutney and Spicy Pear Compote both incorporate this technique.

You'll find many creative ways to use the accompaniments in this chapter to spice up your everyday meals. You might also consider preparing large batches of your favorite condiment for holiday gift-giving or year-round enjoyment.

# Smoked Trout Salad with Celery and Pears

*A variety of distinctive ingredients provides an interesting contrast in texture, color and flavor in this memorable salad. Look for smoked trout at specialty food stores, full-service grocery stores or upscale fish markets.*

*1 bunch frisée or arugula, trimmed, washed and dried*
*2 inner stalks celery, trimmed, sliced on the diagonal
   into 1/4-inch-wide pieces and blanched*
*2 ripe red-skinned pears (preferably Red Bartlett,
   Red Crimson or Red Anjou), quartered, cored
   and thinly sliced crosswise*
*1 whole smoked boneless trout (approximately 1
   pound), head, tail, fins and skin removed, and
   broken into 1/2-inch pieces*

*3 tablespoons mild-flavored olive oil*
*2 tablespoons walnut oil*
*3 tablespoons apple cider vinegar*
*1 bunch fresh chives, cut into 1/2-inch pieces*
*2 tablespoons finely chopped fresh tarragon*
*Salt and freshly ground black pepper, to taste*
*Lemon wedges, for garnish*

Arrange the frisée or arugula on a large platter.

In a medium bowl, combine the celery, pears and trout.

In a small bowl, combine the olive and walnut oils. Slowly add the vinegar, whisking constantly with a wire whisk to form a smooth emulsion. Add the chives and tarragon and mix well. Add to the trout mixture, season with salt and pepper and toss gently. Mound the mixture over the frisée and serve immediately, garnished with the lemon wedges. *Serves 4*

## Warm Green Salad with Pears and Bacon

*When paired with a loaf of warm bread and a chunk of good cheese,
this robustly flavored salad makes a wonderful cool-weather supper. If you
can't find arugula and frisée, substitute escarole and curly endive.*

1 pound bacon
1/4 cup walnut oil
2 1/2 tablespoons balsamic vinegar
1/2 cup fruity olive oil
1 large bunch arugula, trimmed, washed and dried

2 bunches frisée, trimmed, washed and dried
Salt and freshly ground black pepper, to taste
2 large firm-but-ripe pears (preferably Bartlett,
   Anjou or Comice), halved, cored and thinly
   sliced lengthwise

In a large skillet, cook the bacon until crisp. Remove with a slotted spoon and drain on paper towels. Coarsely chop and set aside.

In a very large bowl, combine the walnut oil and balsamic vinegar, whisking constantly with a wire whisk to form a smooth emulsion. Set aside until needed.

In a small saucepan, heat the olive oil over medium-high heat until it just begins to smoke. Add the greens to the bowl containing the walnut oil mixture. Slowly drizzle the hot olive oil over the greens, tossing them constantly with large tongs.

Add the bacon to the warm greens and mix well. Season with salt and pepper. Arrange on individual plates and top with the pears. Serve immediately. *Serves 6*

# Three-Pear and Cucumber Salad with Honey Citrus Dressing

*In this dish, three types of pears and crisp cucumbers are tossed in a honey-laced, bright-tasting citrus vinaigrette to make an invigorating and healthful salad ideal for hot-weather meals.*

**Honey Citrus Dressing:**
*Juice and finely minced zest from 1 lemon*
*Juice and finely minced zest from 1 orange*
*Juice and finely minced zest from 1 lime*
*1/2 cup honey*
*1 1/2 tablespoons poppy seeds*
*1/4 cup finely chopped fresh mint leaves*
*Salt and freshly ground white pepper, to taste*

*2 large Asian pears (preferably Shinseiki or Twentieth Century), halved, cored and cut into 1/2-inch cubes*
*1 ripe red-skinned pear (preferably Red Crimson, Red Blush or Red Anjou), halved, cored and cut into 1/2-inch cubes*
*1 large ripe pear (preferably Bartlett, Comice or Packham), halved, cored and cut into 1/2-inch cubes*
*1/2 English cucumber, peeled, halved lengthwise, seeded and cut into 1/4-inch-wide pieces*
*1 bunch watercress, trimmed, washed and dried, for lining a platter*

To make the dressing, in a large bowl, combine the citrus juices and zests. Slowly add the honey in a thin stream, whisking constantly with a wire whisk to form a smooth emulsion. Add the poppy seeds, mint, salt and pepper and mix well.

Add the pears and cucumber and toss gently. Adjust the seasonings to taste. Arrange on a bed of watercress and serve immediately. *Serves 6*

## Asian Pear and Carrot Slaw with Roasted Peanuts

*Spicy, sweet and piquant, this colorful salad is terrific with barbecued chicken or pork ribs.*

*2 large carrots*
*3 large Asian pears (preferably Shinseiki, Shinko or*
*    Twentieth Century), cored whole and sliced*
*    into 1/8-inch-thick rounds*
*4 scallions, trimmed and sliced on the diagonal into*
*    1/2-inch pieces*
*2 red jalapeño chilies or 1 serrano chili, stemmed,*
*    seeded and thinly sliced*

*2 teaspoons ground coriander*
*1/2 cup peanut oil*
*1/4 cup fresh lemon juice*
*3/4 cup roasted peanuts, coarsely chopped*
*Salt and freshly ground white pepper, to taste*
*1 bunch mizuna, arugula, frisée or watercress,*
*    trimmed, washed and dried, for lining plates*

Using a very sharp chef's knife, cut the carrots on the diagonal into very thin ovals less than 1/8 inch thick and approximately 1 to 1 1/2 inches long. Using 3 slices per pile, stack the carrots into neat bundles. Cutting lengthwise from top to bottom, cut the carrot slices into very thin slivers less than 1/8 inch wide.

In a large pot, bring 6 cups of water to a boil over high heat. Add the carrot slivers and cook 10 seconds. Drain in a colander and rinse under cold water. Lay the slivers on paper towels and pat dry. Set aside.

Using 3 slices per pile, stack the pear rounds into neat bundles. Cut the stacked pears lengthwise into thin strips approximately 1/8 inch wide. Transfer to a large bowl and add the carrots, scallions, chilies and coriander.

In a small bowl place the peanut oil. Slowly add the lemon juice, whisking constantly with a wire whisk to form a smooth emulsion. Just before serving, add to the pear-carrot mixture along with three-fourths of the peanuts. Season with salt and pepper and toss gently. Serve immediately on a bed of greens, garnished with the remaining peanuts. *Serves 6*

## Mixed Greens with Pears and Hazelnuts

*Mild baby lettuces and pleasantly bitter frisée are a perfect foil for two classic autumn ingredients—toasted hazelnuts and juicy, ripe, red-skinned pears. Serve this salad accompanied with bread for a light lunch or as a first course at dinnertime.*

1/2 cup hazelnuts
1/3 cup hazelnut oil
1 clove garlic, minced
2 tablespoons Three-Peppercorn Pear Vinegar
    (see p. 51) or sherry vinegar
1 bunch frisée, trimmed, washed and dried

3 cups mixed baby lettuces, washed and dried
2 ripe red-skinned pears (preferably Red Crimson,
    Red Bartlett or Red Anjou), halved, cored and
    cut into 1/4-inch cubes
Salt and freshly ground black pepper, to taste

Preheat the oven to 350 degrees F.

To remove the papery brown skins from the hazelnuts, arrange in a single layer on a baking sheet. Place in the middle of the oven and bake approximately 7 to 12 minutes, or until the skins turn almost black and begin to flake. Let cool to room temperature. Wrap the nuts in a clean kitchen towel and rub vigor-ously to remove as much of the skins as pos-sible. Coarsely chop and set aside.

In a large bowl, mix the oil and the garlic. Slowly add the vinegar, whisking constantly with a wire whisk to form a smooth emulsion. Add the greens and pears and toss well. Season with salt and pepper. Arrange on individual plates or on a large platter. Garnish with the hazelnuts and serve immediately. *Serves 4 to 6*

# Honey Pear Jam

*If you're in the habit of beginning your day with toasted bread and
fruit preserves, you may want to double this luscious recipe.*

*2 large firm-but-ripe pears (preferably Forelle,
  Bartlett or Comice), halved, cored and cut
  into 1/4-inch cubes*
*1/2 cup water*
*1/4 cup fresh lemon juice*
*1/4 cup pear eau-de-vie*

*1/4 teaspoon ground cinnamon*
*1/4 teaspoon ground cloves*
*1/4 teaspoon ground nutmeg*
*1/2 cup honey*
*Pinch of salt*

In a medium, heavy-bottomed saucepan, combine the pears, water, lemon juice, eau-de-vie and spices; mix well. Bring to a boil over high heat and cook 5 minutes, stirring frequently. Reduce the heat to medium and simmer 25 minutes, stirring occasionally, until almost all the liquid has evaporated and the pears are very tender.

Add the honey and salt and mix well. Cook 15 to 20 minutes, stirring frequently, until the mixture is thick and aromatic and the pears have broken down. Remove from the heat and let cool to room temperature. Transfer to a nonreactive container with a tight-fitting lid and store in the refrigerator for up to 2 months. *Makes approximately 1 cup*

# Pear and Walnut Quick Bread

*This lightly sweetened tender loaf complements hearty foods, such as
roast pork, chicken or turkey, or dishes made with smoked ham or poultry. Spread with
softened cream cheese, it makes a simple but satisfying breakfast offering.
Be sure to use firm, slightly underripe pears for this recipe. If the pears seem too wet once
they are grated, squeeze some of the juice from them before adding to the batter.*

1 3/4 cups granulated sugar
1 cup vegetable oil
3 eggs
Grated zest from 2 lemons
2 teaspoons pure vanilla extract
3 cups all-purpose flour
1 teaspoon salt
1 teaspoon baking soda

1/2 teaspoon baking powder
3/4 teaspoon ground mace
3/4 teaspoon ground cinnamon
4 firm pears (preferably Bosc or Winter Nelis),
    peeled, cored and coarsely grated (approximately
    3 1/2 cups grated)
3/4 cup coarsely chopped walnuts

Preheat the oven to 350 degrees F. Lightly grease two 4 1/2-by-8 1/2-inch loaf pans.

In a large bowl using a hand-held electric mixer, beat the sugar with the oil until the mixture lightens by several shades, approximately 3 minutes. Add the eggs, one at a time, beating well after each addition. Add the lemon zest and vanilla and mix well.

In a small bowl, combine the flour, salt, baking soda, baking powder and spices; mix well. Sprinkle the dry ingredients over the surface of the wet ingredients and fold together, mixing until thoroughly incorporated.

Do not overmix. Add the pears and walnuts and mix until evenly distributed.

Divide the batter evenly between the 2 loaf pans. Bake on the lower shelf of the oven 40 minutes. Transfer to the top shelf and bake 10 minutes longer, or until a toothpick comes out clean when inserted in the center of the breads. Remove from the oven and let cool slightly before removing from the pans. As tempting as it may be, it's best to let the bread cool completely before slicing. The loaf will keep well for several days if securely wrapped and stored at room temperature. *Makes 2 loaves*

## Spicy Pear Compote

*Piquant and aromatic, this chunky pear condiment is terrific with grilled or roasted game, lamb, beef or pork.*

*3 shallots, halved and thinly sliced*
*2 cloves garlic, minced*
*2 teaspoons ground coriander*
*2 teaspoons ground fennel seeds*
*2 teaspoons ground dried red pepper flakes*
*3 tablespoons peanut or vegetable oil*
*1/2 cup dry sherry*
*1/2 cup dried pitted cherries or cranberries*

*4 firm red-skinned pears (preferably Red Crimson,*
 *Red Bartlett or Red Anjou), halved, cored and*
 *cut into 1/2-inch cubes*
*3/4 cup red wine vinegar*
*1/2 cup water*
*1 tablespoon Dijon mustard*
*Salt and freshly ground black pepper, to taste*

In a large, heavy-bottomed saucepan, cook the shallots, garlic and spices in the peanut oil over medium heat 3 minutes, stirring frequently. Add the sherry and cook 5 minutes, or until the liquid has almost evaporated.

 Add the cherries, pears, vinegar, water and mustard; bring to a boil over high heat. Reduce the heat to medium and simmer 25 to 30 minutes, stirring occasionally, until the pears are tender and the mixture is thick and aromatic. Season with salt and pepper and let cool to room temperature. Transfer to a non-reactive container with a tight-fitting lid and store in the refrigerator for up to 3 weeks. Bring to room temperature before serving.
*Makes approximately 3 cups*

## Fiery East Indian Pear Chutney

*Don't let the rather daunting list of ingredients deter you from making this intoxicating chutney.*
*It takes less than ten minutes to prepare all of the components and cooks on the stove for less than one hour.*
*Serve with grilled meats, poultry or sausages, or as a condiment with Indian food.*

1 large red onion, cut into small dice
3 cloves garlic, minced
2 red jalapeño chilies or 1 serrano chili, stemmed,
    seeded and finely chopped
2-inch piece fresh ginger, peeled and finely chopped
1 tablespoon whole yellow mustard seeds
1 teaspoon ground coriander
1 teaspoon ground cumin
1 teaspoon ground fennel seeds
1 teaspoon ground anise
1/2 teaspoon ground cardamom
1/2 teaspoon ground fenugreek

1/2 teaspoon ground cayenne pepper
1/4 teaspoon ground cloves
1/4 teaspoon ground cinnamon
1/4 teaspoon ground mace
3 tablespoons peanut oil
1/2 cup water
1/2 cup finely chopped dried pears
2 large firm pears (preferably Bartlett, Forelle or
    Anjou), halved, cored and cut into
      1/4-inch cubes
1/2 cup fresh lime juice
Salt and freshly ground black pepper, to taste

In a large, heavy-bottomed sauté pan, cook the onion, garlic, chilies, ginger and spices in the peanut oil over medium-high heat 5 to 7 minutes, stirring constantly.

Add the water, dried and fresh pears and lime juice. Bring to a boil over high heat, stirring constantly. Reduce the heat to medium and cook, stirring frequently, 20 to 25 minutes, until the mixture is thick and aromatic. Season with salt and pepper and remove from the heat. Let cool to room temperature. Transfer to a container with a tight-fitting lid and store in the refrigerator for up to 3 weeks. *Makes approximately 2 1/2 cups*

## Cooling Pear and Yogurt Chutney with Mint

*Inspired by a traditional East Indian chutney, this version, with its inclusion of finely shredded pears, provides a welcome counterbalance to hot, spicy Indian dishes. It also goes nicely with grilled poultry and fish and works well as a topping for spicy grain and vegetable dishes.*

1 1/2 cups plain low-fat yogurt
3 tablespoons fresh lemon juice
1/3 cup finely chopped fresh mint leaves
3 tablespoons finely chopped fresh cilantro leaves
1 firm-but-ripe pear (preferably Comice,
    Winter Nelis or Bosc), peeled, cored and
    finely shredded
Salt and freshly ground white pepper, to taste

In a nonreactive bowl, combine the yogurt, lemon juice, mint, cilantro and pear; mix gently. Season with salt and pepper. Transfer to a container with a tight-fitting lid and store in the refrigerator for up to 1 1/2 weeks. *Makes approximately 2 cups*

## Three-Peppercorn Pear Vinegar

*Whether sprinkled on fresh fruit, added to soups, stews and stir-fried dishes, or used in vinaigrettes, this peppery-sweet, pear-scented vinegar complements a wide variety of foods, both sweet and savory.*

3 cups champagne vinegar
1 cup rice wine vinegar
1 teaspoon whole black peppercorns
1 teaspoon whole white peppercorns
1 teaspoon whole green peppercorns
6 red jalapeño or 3 serrano chilies, stemmed
2 firm-but-ripe pears (preferably Red Crimson,
    Anjou or Bartlett), cored and coarsely chopped

In a large, nonreactive bowl, combine the vinegars, peppercorns, chilies and pears; mix well. Transfer to a large nonreactive bottle with a tight-fitting lid and refrigerate for at least 2 weeks or up to 1 month.

Strain once through a fine wire sieve lined with several layers of cheesecloth; discard the solids and the cheesecloth. Line the sieve with several layers of clean cheesecloth. Strain the liquid three or four more times, replacing the soiled cheesecloth with clean layers each time, until the vinegar is absolutely clear.

Transfer to a clean, nonreactive container with a tight-fitting lid and store in the refrigerator for up to 6 months. *Makes approximately 2 cups*

*Left to right: Cooling Pear and Yogurt Chutney with Mint, Three-Peppercorn Pear Vinegar and Fiery East Indian Pear Chutney (recipe p. 49)*

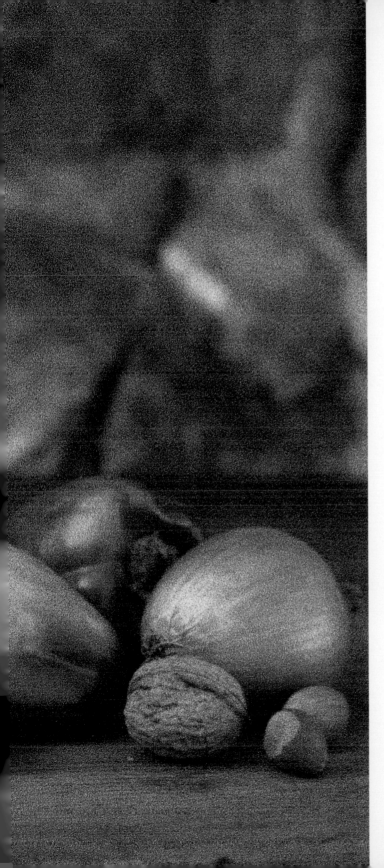

# MAIN COURSES

Historically, the custom of combining fresh or dried fruits with savory ingredients is prevalent in almost every cuisine of the world. It is especially widespread in the Middle East, parts of the Soviet Union, the Baltic countries, Northern Europe, India, and to a lesser degree, the Mediterranean and Africa. The recipes in this chapter borrow from these culinary traditions.

Frequently joined with pork, pears make a nice counter-balance to duck and chicken dishes as well. They also combine unexpectedly well with seafood, particularly mild-tasting, meaty fish, which the Wine-Poached Salmon with Pears and Shallots beautifully demonstrates. And they provide a refreshing contrast to the richness of cheese dishes, as the Pasta Shells with Pears and Gorgonzola Cream illustrates.

These main course dishes highlight the chameleon nature of pears; depending on the accompanying ingredients in a recipe, pears can seem very sugary and fruity, while in others they have a barely sweet, almost vegetable-like quality. In many of these recipes, the pears are quickly sautéed in the liquid or oil remaining after the other ingredients are cooked. This brief cooking preserves the shape, texture and flavor of the fruit, ensuring that its appealing qualities shine through.

## Wine-Poached Salmon with Pears and Shallots

*When the heat is on and you have no time to fuss over cooking, make this elegant salmon dish for a formal lunch or a light supper. Serve on a bed of mixed baby lettuces or braised greens for a complete meal.*

*4 cups dry white wine*
*4 shallots, finely chopped*
*1 bay leaf*
*4 salmon steaks (approximately 8 ounces each)*
*2 firm-but-ripe pears (preferably Bartlett, Packham*
*    or Comice), peeled, halved, cored and cut into*
*    1/4-inch cubes*

*Salt and freshly ground white pepper, to taste*
*Mixed baby lettuces, to line a platter*
*Parsley sprigs, for garnish*

In a large, shallow saucepan, bring the wine, shallots and bay leaf to a boil over high heat. Cook 3 minutes, stirring from time to time. Add the salmon and return to a boil. (If there isn't enough liquid to cover the salmon, add just enough hot water to cover the steaks.) Immediately reduce the heat to medium, cover the saucepan with a tight-fitting lid and simmer 5 or 6 minutes, or until the surface of the salmon is dotted with small, cream-colored spots of liquid and the center of the steaks are just opaque. Remove the salmon with a slotted spatula, reserving the cooking liquid, and set aside until needed. Remove the bay leaf and discard.

In the same pan, bring the poaching liquid to a boil over high heat and cook 6 or 7 minutes, or until reduced to approximately 1 cup. Add the pears, reduce the heat to medium and cook 3 minutes, or until tender. Season with salt and pepper. Arrange the baby lettuces on individual plates or a large platter and top with the salmon. Spoon the pears and a little of the liquid over the top of each salmon steak. Serve immediately garnished with the parsley.
*Serves 4*

# Pasta with Bay Scallops, Pears and Coppa

*The combined flavors of sweet bay scallops, smoky, hot coppa and fresh pears in
this unique dish will ignite the taste buds. Coppa—cured and spiced pork shoulder—can be found
in Italian delicatessens, full-service grocery stores and most specialty food shops.*

*2 shallots, halved and thinly sliced*
*2 cloves garlic, minced*
*1/2 cup fruity olive oil*
*1 pound penne pasta*
*3/4 pound bay scallops, small side muscles removed*
*1/3 pound medium-sliced spicy coppa, coarsely
    chopped*

*3 firm-but-ripe green-skinned pears (preferably
    Packham, Bartlett or Anjou), halved,
    cored and cut into 1/4-inch cubes*
*1/3 cup fresh lemon juice*
*1 1/2 teaspoons finely chopped fresh thyme*
*1/3 cup finely chopped parsley*
*Salt and freshly ground black pepper, to taste*

In a very large, nonstick sauté pan; cook the shallots and garlic in 1/4 cup of the olive oil over medium heat 5 minutes, stirring occasionally. Remove from the heat and set aside.

In an 8-quart pot, bring 6 quarts of salted water to a boil. Add the pasta and cook 10 or 11 minutes, or until al dente. Drain well in a colander and place in a large bowl. Add the remaining 1/4 cup olive oil and toss well. Place in a warm oven until needed.

To the shallot-garlic mixture add the scallops, coppa and pears and cook 2 minutes, stirring constantly, until the scallops are just cooked through and the pears are tender. Add the lemon juice and thyme and cook 10 seconds. Immediately add to the pasta along with the parsley. Toss well, season with salt and pepper and serve immediately. *Serves 6*

# Pasta Shells with Pears and Gorgonzola Cream

*Present this decadent and flavorful pasta dish to those passionate about blue cheese*
*and dispassionate about calories and fat. If you can't find imported dolcelatte cheese, also known*
*as Gorgonzola dolce, use a mild, creamy, high-quality blue cheese instead.*

2/3 cup walnuts
3 cups heavy cream
3 cloves garlic, minced
1/2 teaspoon dried hot red pepper flakes
3 large ripe red-skinned pears (preferably Red
    Crimson, Red Bartlett or Red Anjou), halved,
    cored and cut into 1/2-inch cubes

2/3 pound imported Gorgonzola cheese, preferably
    dolcelatte (rind removed), crumbled
1 pound medium-sized pasta shells
1 1/2 teaspoons finely chopped fresh thyme
1 teaspoon finely chopped fresh rosemary
Salt and freshly ground black pepper, to taste
1/2 cup finely chopped fresh chives, for garnish

Preheat the oven to 350 degrees F.

Arrange the walnuts in a single layer on a baking sheet. Place in the middle of the oven and bake 7 to 8 minutes, or until nuts are light golden brown and aromatic. Let cool, then coarsely chop and set aside.

In a very large, deep-sided sauté pan, place the cream, garlic and red pepper flakes. Bring to a boil over high heat and cook 7 minutes, stirring constantly to prevent the cream from boiling over. Reduce the heat to medium and cook 10 to 15 minutes, stirring frequently, or until the mixture is thick enough to coat the back of a spoon. Add the pears and cheese and mix gently. Remove from the heat and set aside until needed.

In an 8-quart pot, bring 6 quarts of salted water to a boil over high heat. Add the pasta and cook 10 or 11 minutes, or until al dente. Drain well in a colander and place in a very large bowl. Reheat the cream mixture over high heat, stirring constantly, until thick and bubbling and the cheese has completely melted. Add to the pasta along with the walnuts, thyme and rosemary; toss gently. Season with salt and pepper. Garnish with the chives and serve immediately. *Serves 6*

# Roast Cornish Game Hens with Pear and Cornbread Stuffing

*This recipe makes enough stuffing for eight Cornish game hens. When preparing fewer than eight birds, transfer the extra stuffing to a lightly greased casserole dish and either cover tightly with tin foil and freeze for later use or bake separately in a 350 degree F. oven for 30 to 35 minutes, or until thoroughly heated. Serve along with the stuffed birds as a side dish.*

**Stuffing:**
*1 medium yellow onion, cut into small dice*
*2 cloves garlic, minced*
*1 tablespoon ground coriander*
*4 tablespoons (1/2 stick) unsalted butter*
*3 tablespoons fruity olive oil*

*3 firm pears (preferably Bosc, Winter Nelis or Forelle), halved, cored and cut into 1/4-inch cubes*
*2 1/2 cups cubed store-bought cornbread stuffing*
*1 cup dry white wine*
*Salt and freshly ground black pepper, to taste*

*8 Cornish game hens, insides patted dry*

To make the stuffing, in a very large, nonstick sauté pan, cook the onion, garlic and coriander in the butter and olive oil over medium heat for 7 minutes, stirring frequently, or until the onions are soft.

Add the pears and cook over high heat 3 minutes, stirring constantly. Stir in the store-bought cornbread stuffing and the wine and mix well. Lower the heat to medium and cook an additional 7 or 8 minutes, stirring occasionally with a fork, until the stuffing is moist and the pears are almost tender. Remove from the heat and season generously with salt and pepper. Let cool to room temperature before stuffing the hens.

Preheat the oven to 450 degrees F.

Using approximately 3/4 cup of stuffing per hen, loosely fill the cavity of each hen. (Do not tightly pack the stuffing inside the birds because it expands as it cooks.) Using toothpicks or a trussing needle and heavy thread, close the opening on each hen.

Lightly grease a roasting pan large enough to accommodate all the birds. (If your pan is too small for all 8 birds you may have to use 2 pans; rotate them between the oven shelves to ensure even cooking.) Place a large, flat roasting rack inside the roasting pan and set the birds, breast side down, on the rack.

Place in the lower third of the oven and roast 15 minutes. Reduce the heat to 350 degrees F. Remove the pan from the oven and turn the hens over so the breast sides are facing upward. Return to the oven and roast 20 to 25 minutes, or until the leg juices run clear when pierced with a sharp knife. Remove from the oven and let stand 5 minutes before serving.
*Serves 8*

# Chicken Sauté with Pears and Red Bell Peppers

*This spicy, colorful mélange of fruit, vegetables and chicken is lovely served on a large platter
surrounded by steamed rice, tossed with cooked pasta or cracked wheat, or atop a bed of mixed greens.*

*3 shallots, halved and thinly sliced*
*2 cloves garlic, minced*
*2 teaspoons ground coriander*
*1 teaspoon ground fenugreek*
*2 tablespoons fruity olive oil*
*1 tablespoon unsalted butter*
*2 boneless, skinless chicken breasts, sliced into*
   *1/2-inch-wide pieces*

*1 large red bell pepper, stemmed, seeded and cut into*
   *1/2-inch-wide pieces*
*1 large firm pear (preferably Packham, Anjou or*
   *Bosc), quartered, cored and sliced into*
   *1/4-inch-thick pieces*
*1/3 cup pear eau-de-vie*
*2 tablespoons Three-Peppercorn Pear Vinegar*
   *(see p. 51) or sherry vinegar*
*Salt and freshly ground black pepper, to taste*

In a large sauté pan, cook the shallots, garlic and spices in the olive oil and butter over medium-high heat 3 minutes, stirring frequently. Add the chicken, bell pepper, pear and eau-de-vie. Cook 4 or 5 minutes, stirring constantly, until the chicken is just done and the liquid has evaporated. Add the vinegar and season with salt and pepper; mix well. Serve immediately. *Serves 4*

# Roast Duck Breast with Balsamic Pears

*Splashes of balsamic vinegar and pear eau-de-vie create a rich glaze
that enhances the delicate flavor of duck and fresh pears in this memorable dish.*

4 boneless duck breasts (approximately 8 ounces each),
   skin removed and reserved
2 shallots, halved and thinly sliced
2 firm pears (preferably Bosc or Winter Nelis),
   peeled, cored and finely chopped

1 teaspoon ground fennel seeds
1/4 cup pear eau-de-vie
1/4 cup balsamic vinegar
Salt and freshly ground black pepper, to taste
Fresh rosemary or oregano sprigs, for garnish

Preheat the oven to 425 degrees F.

Place the duck breasts in a lightly greased shallow baking pan. Roast on the top shelf of the oven approximately 5 minutes. Remove and set aside until needed.

Meanwhile, in a large, nonstick sauté pan, cook the duck skin over medium heat 3 minutes, or until approximately 3 tablespoons of fat is rendered. Remove the skins and discard.

In the same pan, cook the shallots, pears and fennel seeds in the duck fat over high heat 2 minutes, stirring frequently. Add the eau-de-vie and balsamic vinegar and cook over high heat approximately 3 minutes, stirring frequently, until the mixture is slightly thick and the pears are tender. Remove from the heat and season with salt and pepper.

Evenly distribute the pear-shallot mixture among 4 individual plates or on a large platter. Thinly slice each duck breast and place on top of the pears. Garnish with the fresh herb sprigs and serve immediately. *Serves 4*

# Roast Pork Tenderloin with Asian Pears and Prunes

*This is a good dish to make for company as it serves six to eight people
and requires little attention. You can prepare the pear and prune mixture a day
in advance, leaving just the cooking of the pork for the last minute.*

*2 shallots, halved and thinly sliced*
*2 cloves garlic, minced*
*1/2 teaspoon ground star anise*
*1/2 teaspoon ground coriander*
*1/2 teaspoon ground caraway seeds*
*4 tablespoons mild-flavored olive oil*
*9 pitted prunes, finely chopped*

*2 Asian pears (preferably Shinseiki or Twentieth
    Century), peeled, halved, cored and cut into
    1/4-inch cubes*
*1/3 cup pear eau-de-vie*
*2 pork tenderloins (approximately 2/3 pound each),
    trimmed of fat and tendon*
*Salt and freshly ground black pepper, to taste*

Preheat the oven to 450 degrees F. Lightly grease a 9-inch baking pan.

In a large, nonstick sauté pan, cook the shallots, garlic and spices in 3 tablespoons of the olive oil over medium heat 3 minutes, stirring frequently. Add the prunes, pears and eau-de-vie and cook over high heat 2 minutes, stirring constantly. Reduce the heat to medium and cook 10 to 12 minutes, stirring occasionally, until the pears are very tender and the mixture is slightly thick. Transfer to the prepared baking pan.

Rub the tenderloins with the remaining tablespoon of olive oil and place on top of the pear-prune mixture. Sprinkle with salt and pepper.

Roast on the top shelf of the oven 18 to 20 minutes, or until the interior is barely pink and the internal temperature reaches 150 degrees F. on a meat thermometer. Remove from the oven and let stand at room temperature 5 minutes before cutting into 1-inch-thick slices. Serve with the pear-prune mixture alongside or underneath. *Serves 6 to 8*

# SWEETS

Pears are right at home in sweet concoctions—this is where we most expect to find them. Fresh, healthful and light, they are sophisticated in an understated way. At once mellow and distinctive, juicy and crisp, pears lend an appealing texture and flavor to a wide range of desserts, both classic and contemporary.

Many of the dishes in this section are traditional recipes that have been updated to showcase pears in a more compelling fashion. You will be treated to such classics as Baked Pears with Warm Caramel or Chocolate Sauce, Caramelized Pear Galette and Spiced Pear Cake with Vanilla Whipped Cream. In addition to these familiar and comforting sweets are new and unique recipes using European and Asian pears as the starring ingredients. Elegant Cinnamon-Scented Date and Pear Phyllo Rolls, Asian Pears with Spiced Sweet Coconut Cream and Minted Pear Sorbet are among the offerings.

These desserts range from down-home to truly refined, and from refreshingly light to outrageously decadent; they will polish off any meal in style. But if your time is minimal and whipping up a tart or pie isn't possible, don't despair. For true pear lovers, as a perfect finale nothing compares to the simplicity and purity of a single succulent, sweet and juicy, ripe pear, eaten out of hand.

# Crustless Almond and Pear Tart

*Infused with the essence of almonds, this winning pear tart is bound together with a cake-like batter that replaces the traditional crust. It is very easy to make and keeps well at room temperature for up to four days. Serve plain for breakfast or brunch or with whipped cream or crème fraîche for dessert.*

6 1/2 tablespoons unsalted butter
1 1/4 cups whole almonds
2/3 cup plus 2 tablespoons granulated sugar
1/2 cup all-purpose flour
1/2 teaspoon ground mace
1/2 teaspoon ground cinnamon
1/2 teaspoon ground nutmeg

1/4 teaspoon salt
2 eggs, lightly beaten
2 tablespoons pear eau-de-vie
1/4 cup whole milk
1 vanilla pod, split lengthwise and seeds removed
2 firm-but-ripe pears (preferably Anjou, Bartlett or
       Red Blush), quartered and cored

Preheat the oven to 350 degrees F. Generously grease a fluted 9 1/2-by-1-inch ceramic baking dish or tart pan.

In a small saucepan, melt 5 tablespoons of the butter over low heat until melted. Remove from heat, let cool to room temperature and set aside until needed. Cut the remaining 1 1/2 tablespoons of butter into small pieces and set aside until needed.

Place the almonds and 2/3 cup of the sugar in a food processor fitted with the metal blade. Process, pulsing on and off, until finely ground. Do not overprocess or the mixture will form a paste. Transfer to a large bowl and add the flour, spices and salt. Mix well.

In a small bowl, combine the eggs, eau-de-vie, milk, vanilla seeds and the reserved melted butter and mix well. Add to the dry ingredients and mix thoroughly. Pour the batter into the prepared dish or pan and smooth the surface.

Using a sharp knife, cut the pears crosswise into 1/8-inch-wide slices, keeping the slices together as you go. One quarter at a time, slide the pears onto a narrow spatula or palette knife and set on top of the batter with the smaller (neck) end of the pear in the center and the wider end toward the outer edge—like the spokes of a wheel. Arrange all the pears in this fashion and gently press into the batter so that only the surface of the pears is exposed. Sprinkle with the remaining 2 tablespoons of sugar and scatter the butter pieces over the top.

Bake on the lower shelf of the oven 10 minutes. Rotate to the upper shelf and bake 30 to 35 minutes longer, or until the batter is puffy and golden brown. Let cool slightly and serve warm, or cool completely and serve at room temperature. *Serves 8*

## Sautéed Pears with Pear Eau-de-Vie Brown Butter Sauce

*Simple yet elegant, this dessert is easy to prepare and contains few ingredients, making it a good last-minute dish to serve when pressed for time. For a more elegant finale, serve these sumptuous pears over vanilla ice cream or with homemade pound cake.*

5 tablespoons unsalted butter
1/2 teaspoon ground nutmeg
3 large ripe pears (preferably Bartlett, Comice or
    Anjou), peeled, halved, cored and cut into
    1/2-inch slices
1/2 cup firmly packed dark brown sugar
1/2 cup pear eau-de-vie
Pinch freshly ground white pepper
Mint sprigs, for garnish
Crème fraîche, for garnish

In a very large nonstick sauté pan, melt the butter with the nutmeg over medium heat. Add the pears and cook over high heat 2 minutes, stirring frequently.

Add the sugar, eau-de-vie and pepper (stand back from the pan because the eau-de-vie will ignite). Allow the flames to die down before stirring the mixture. Cook 3 minutes, stirring constantly, until the sauce is thick and dark brown. Remove from the heat, spoon into shallow bowls and serve immediately, garnished with mint sprigs and dollops of crème fraîche. *Serves 4 to 6*

## Vanilla-Poached Fresh and Dried Pears

*The warm, inviting scent of fresh pears, cinnamon and vanilla beans simmering in white wine is welcome any time of the year, but I like to serve this comforting dessert when the leaves begin to change color and the air is crisp.*

3 cups dry white wine
1 cup sweet sherry
2 cups water
1/2 cup granulated sugar
3 vanilla pods, split lengthwise and seeds removed
2 cinnamon sticks
1 teaspoon ground nutmeg
6 small firm pears (preferably Summer Gold or
    French Butter), left whole, peeled and cored
1/2 cup finely chopped dried pears
1/2 cup golden raisins
Mint sprigs, for garnish

In a heavy-bottomed 6-quart saucepan, place the wine, sherry, water, sugar, vanilla pods and seeds, cinnamon sticks and nutmeg. Bring to a boil over high heat and cook 10 minutes, stirring frequently. Reduce the heat to medium-high and cook 20 minutes, stirring occasionally, until the liquid has reduced by one third and its aroma fills the air.

Add the fresh and dried pears and golden raisins. Simmer over medium heat 15 to 20 minutes, stirring occasionally, until the fresh pears are just tender. Remove from the heat. Remove the vanilla pods and cinnamon sticks and discard. Serve the warm pears in shallow bowls with some of the poaching liquid, garnished with the mint. *Serves 6*

*Vanilla-Poached Fresh and Dried Pears*

# Baked Pears with Warm Caramel or Chocolate Sauce

*I prefer the seductive, buttery flavor of caramel sauce with baked pears, but for
die-hard chocoholics, I have included a recipe for chocolate sauce as well. If you would like to
really "gild the lily," you can serve the baked pears with a drizzle of both sauces.*

4 large firm-but-ripe pears (preferably Bartlett,
    Red Crimson or Packham), peeled, halved
    and cored
3/4 cup lemon juice

**Warm Caramel Sauce:**
6 tablespoons unsalted butter
1/2 cup firmly packed dark brown sugar
1 cup heavy cream

**Chocolate Sauce:**
1 cup heavy cream
8 ounces bittersweet chocolate, coarsely chopped
1/4 cup granulated sugar
2 teaspoons pure vanilla extract

1/2 cup pecans, for garnish
Mint sprigs, for garnish

Preheat the oven to 400 degrees F.

Place the pears in a large bowl with the lemon juice. Toss gently to coat all sides. Remove the pears and arrange, cut sides down, in a shallow baking pan large enough to accommodate all the fruit in a single layer. Add any remaining lemon juice and enough hot water to reach a level of 1/4 inch. Bake approximately 15 minutes, or until the pears are tender but not mushy. Remove with a slotted spoon and set aside until needed.

To make the warm caramel sauce, in a medium, heavy-bottomed saucepan, melt the butter with the sugar over medium heat, stirring frequently to prevent the butter from burning. Cook 3 minutes, or until the sugar has dissolved and the mixture is foamy. Slowly add the cream, whisking constantly to prevent the mixture from boiling over. Cook approximately 8 or 9 minutes, stirring frequently, until the sauce is thick and creamy. Keep warm.

To make the chocolate sauce, in the top of a double boiler set over simmering water, place the cream, chocolate and sugar. Cook over medium heat, stirring frequently, until the sauce is thick and aromatic and the sugar has completely dissolved. Add the vanilla and mix well. Keep warm.

Lower the heat to 350 degrees F. Arrange pecans in a single layer on a baking sheet. Place in the middle of the oven and bake approximately 6 to 7 minutes, or until nuts are light golden brown and aromatic. Let cool, then finely chop.

To serve, place 2 pear halves on each individual serving plate and spoon one or both sauces over the top. (If you wish to serve the pears hot or warm, either slightly underbake them initially and reheat just before serving, or serve them straight from the oven.) Sprinkle with the pecans and garnish with the mint sprigs. Serve immediately. *Serves 4*

## Asian Pears with Spiced Sweet Coconut Cream

*Warm, sweet spices and rich coconut milk lend a sultry Asian flavor to this distinctive dessert.*
*It is especially good as a late-night snack on cold winter nights or as an unusual breakfast dish.*

*Two 15-ounce cans sweetened coconut cream*
*2 star anise*
*1 teaspoon ground cinnamon*
*1 teaspoon ground nutmeg*
*1 teaspoon ground allspice*

*3 Asian pears (preferably Shinseiki or*
*Twentieth Century), peeled, halved,*
*cored and cut into eighths*
*1/3 cup shredded coconut, lightly toasted,*
*for garnish*

In a large, heavy-bottomed saucepan, place the coconut milk, spices and pears. Bring to a boil over high heat, stirring frequently.

Reduce the heat to medium and simmer 30 minutes, stirring occasionally, until the pears are tender but not mushy. Remove from the heat. Ladle the warm pears into small bowls with some of the coconut cream. Garnish with the toasted coconut and serve immediately.
*Serves 6*

# Pear Upside-Down Cake

*This version of a cake traditionally made with pineapples is extremely moist,*
*flavorful and tender. Garnish with a dollop of whipped cream, vanilla yogurt or crème fraîche.*
*The cake is also delectable served unadorned for breakfast or snacks.*

*16 tablespoons (1/2 pound) unsalted butter,*
*    softened to room temperature*
*3/4 cup granulated sugar*
*3 eggs*
*1 vanilla bean, split lengthwise and seeds removed*
*1/2 cup whole milk*
*1 1/2 cups all-purpose flour*

*1 1/2 teaspoons baking powder*
*1/2 teaspoon ground nutmeg*
*1 cup tightly packed light brown sugar*
*4 small firm-but-ripe pears (preferably French Butter,*
*    Seckel or Summer Gold), peeled, halved, cored*
*    and cut into sixths*
*3 tablespoons pear eau-de-vie*

Preheat the oven to 375 degrees F.

In a large bowl using an electric mixer, beat 12 tablespoons of the butter until pale and creamy, approximately 2 minutes. Add the sugar and beat until light and fluffy, 2 to 3 minutes. Add the eggs, one at a time, beating well after each addition. Add the vanilla seeds and milk and mix well. Sprinkle the flour, baking powder and nutmeg over the surface of the wet ingredients. Fold in until thoroughly incorporated. Set aside until needed.

In a 12-inch, heavy-bottomed, oven-proof sauté pan, melt the remaining 4 tablespoons of butter over low heat. When melted, add the brown sugar and cook over medium heat 3 to 5 minutes, stirring frequently, until the sugar dissolves and the mixture is bubbly. Add the sliced pears and eau-de-vie and cook over medium-high heat approximately 5 to 7 minutes, stirring frequently, or until the pears are slightly tender and the butter-sugar mixture is thick and bubbly. Remove from the heat.

Using a tablespoon, evenly distribute the batter over the pear mixture in the sauté pan and quickly spread it into an even, smooth layer. Bake on the lower shelf of the oven 20 minutes, or until a toothpick inserted into the center of the cake portion comes out clean. Remove from the oven and let cool 10 minutes before unmolding.

To unmold, run a dull knife between the cake and the edge of the pan, gently pulling it away from the sides. Place a large platter over the cake. Quickly invert the cake onto the platter. Serve warm or at room temperature.
*Serves 10 to 12*

# Spiced Pear Cake with Vanilla Whipped Cream

*A variety of aromatic spices adds depth to this tender layer cake infused with pears.*
*Since it actually improves in flavor the second day, feel free to prepare the cake one day*
*ahead, wrap it tightly in plastic wrap and store at room temperature. Within an hour*
*before serving, make the vanilla whipped cream and assemble the cake.*

**Spiced Pear Cake:**
2 1/2 cups all-purpose flour
3/4 cup granulated sugar
1/2 cup tightly packed light brown sugar
2 teaspoons baking powder
1 teaspoon baking soda
2 teaspoons ground cinnamon
1/2 teaspoon ground mace
1/2 teaspoon ground nutmeg
1/2 teaspoon ground allspice
1/2 teaspoon ground kosher salt
1/4 teaspoon ground anise seeds
1/4 teaspoon ground cloves
3 eggs, lightly beaten

1 cup sour cream
6 tablespoons unsalted butter, melted and cooled
3 tablespoons pear eau-de-vie
4 small ripe pears (preferably Seckel, Italian Butter
    or Summer Gold), peeled, halved, cored and
    cut into 1/4-inch cubes (approximately 3
    cups cubed)

**Vanilla Whipped Cream:***
2 cups well-chilled heavy cream
1 vanilla pod, split lengthwise and seeds removed
1/2 cup powdered sugar, sifted
1 1/2 tablespoons pear eau-de-vie

*Mint sprigs, for garnish*

To make the cake, preheat the oven to 350 degrees F. Generously butter two 8-inch cake pans. Dust with flour and set aside until needed.

    In a large bowl, combine the flour, white and brown sugars, baking powder, baking soda and spices; mix well.

    In another large bowl, combine the eggs and sour cream, whisking vigorously to form a smooth mixture. Add the butter and eau-de-vie and mix well. Add the dry ingredients to the wet ingredients, mixing gently until thoroughly combined. Add the pears and mix well. The batter will be fairly stiff.

    Divide the batter between the two prepared cake pans. Place on the bottom shelf of the oven and bake 35 to 40 minutes, or until a toothpick comes out clean when inserted in the centers of the cakes. Remove from the oven and let cool to room temperature before removing from the pan. When cool, run a dull knife around the edges of each cake, gently

loosening them from the sides and bottoms of the pans. Place one layer on a large plate, reserving the second layer.

To make the vanilla whipped cream, in a large bowl, place the cream and the vanilla seeds. Using an electric mixer, beat the cream until soft peaks form. Add the sugar and beat until very stiff, but not dry. Add the eau-de-vie and beat until the cream is stiff enough to hold its shape between the two layers of cake.

To assemble the cake, spread half of the whipped cream over the top of the plated bottom layer of cake. Gently top with the second cake layer and spread the top with the remaining whipped cream. Garnish with mint sprigs and serve immediately. *Makes 1 double-layer cake*

*Note:* The recipe for vanilla whipped cream makes just enough to cover the middle and top layer. If you prefer a cake completely cloaked in whipped cream, double the recipe.

# Old-Fashioned Pear and Apricot Pie with Ginger

*Pears are available year-round, but apricots are a summer fruit, so make this pie during the warm-weather months.*

**Crust:**
1 1/2 cups all-purpose flour
2 tablespoons granulated sugar
3/4 teaspoon kosher salt
1/2 cup tightly packed chilled solid vegetable
    shortening
3 to 4 tablespoons ice water

**Filling:**
5 firm-but-ripe apricots, pitted and quartered

8 medium firm-but-ripe pears (preferably Red
    Crimson, Anjou or Comice), halved, cored and
    cut lengthwise into 1/2-inch wedges
2-inch piece fresh ginger, peeled and finely minced
Juice from 1 lemon
1/3 cup granulated sugar
3 tablespoons cornstarch
1 teaspoon ground cinnamon
Pinch of salt and freshly ground black pepper
2 tablespoons unsalted butter, cut into 6 pieces

To make the crust, in a large bowl, combine the flour, sugar and salt. Add the shortening in small pieces. Working quickly, using brisk, rapid movements with your fingers, combine the shortening with the dry ingredients until the mixture resembles coarse meal. Add just enough of the ice water to form the mixture into a cohesive ball. If the dough is too crumbly, add more ice water, 1 tablespoon at a time.

Form the dough into a flat disc, wrap tightly in plastic and refrigerate for at least 1 hour or up to 1 day. (If refrigerated longer than 1 hour, remove from the refrigerator 30 minutes before rolling.)

Preheat the oven to 400 degrees F.

On a lightly floured surface, roll the dough into a thin, even circle approximately 1/8 inch thick. Gently fold the dough in half and place in a lightly greased 9-inch pie pan. Unfold and center the dough. Using a sharp paring knife, trim the edges of the dough so that it hangs evenly 1 inch over the rim of the pan. Turn the edge of the dough down over itself toward the inside of the pan, making an even, raised ridge around the rim. Form into an attractive edge by crimping the ridge with your fingers. Refrigerate for 30 minutes before baking.

Line the pastry shell with parchment paper or foil. Add pie weights, dried beans or rice. Bake on the lower shelf of the oven 15 minutes. Remove pie weights and liner and bake 7 minutes longer. Remove from the oven and let cool to room temperature before filling.

To make the filling, in a large bowl, place the apricots, pears, ginger, lemon juice, sugar, cornstarch, cinnamon, salt and pepper. Gently combine the ingredients, taking care not to break the fruit. Spoon the filling into the cooled pastry shell and dot the top with the butter.

Bake on the lower shelf of the oven 50 to 55 minutes, or until the fruit is tender and the crust is golden brown. Remove from the oven and let stand at room temperature 20 to 30 minutes to allow the juices to thicken. Slice into wedges and serve immediately. *Makes 1 pie*

# Basmati Rice Pudding with Pears and Blueberries

*Rice pudding is the ultimate comfort food. This version combines basmati rice, which has
a sweet, exotic and delicate quality, and Asian pears and blueberries, which add texture and color.*

1 cup basmati or jasmine rice
7 to 8 cups whole milk★
1 teaspoon ground nutmeg
1/2 cup granulated sugar
2 Asian pears (preferably Shinseiki, Twentieth
    Century or Yoinashi), halved, cored and cut
    into small dice

Minced zest from 1 medium lemon
Pinch of kosher salt
1 cup fresh or frozen blueberries
1 1/2 tablespoons fresh lemon juice
2/3 cup finely chopped toasted pistachios, for garnish
    (optional)

In a large, heavy-bottomed saucepan, place the rice, 6 cups of the milk and the nutmeg. Bring to a boil over high heat. Reduce the heat to medium-low and simmer 15 minutes, stirring frequently.

Add the sugar, pears, lemon zest, salt and remaining 1 cup of milk (add frozen blueberries, if using, at this time). Cook 10 to 12 minutes, stirring occasionally, until the rice is very tender and the pears are tender but not mushy. Add the lemon juice and the fresh blueberries, if using, at this time; mix gently and remove from the heat. Serve warm or at room temperature, garnished with the pistachios, if desired.

The pudding can also be cooled to room temperature and stored in a tightly sealed container in the refrigerator for up to 5 days. The pudding can be eaten chilled or reheated. To reheat, place in a heavy-bottomed saucepan with a small amount of water or milk and heat over a low flame until warmed through. *Serves 6 to 8*

*★Note:* Different kinds of rice (even different bags of the same type) absorb liquids at a different rate. If your pudding looks too dry, or if the rice doesn't seem within 12 minutes of being fully cooked as the last cup of milk is added, add another half or whole cup of milk.

# Cinnamon-Scented Date and Pear Phyllo Rolls

*Best served hot from the oven, this marvelous dessert needs only a garnish of fresh mint sprigs to finish it off.*
*The filling is best made a day ahead, but try to assemble the phyllo rolls less than one hour prior to baking.*

**Filling:**
2 Asian pears (preferably Shinseiki or Twentieth
    Century), halved, cored and finely chopped
8 ounces pitted dates, coarsely chopped
Juice from 1 orange
1 teaspoon ground cinnamon
1/2 cup pear eau-de-vie

1/4 cup water
Dash freshly ground white pepper

12 to 15 sheets phyllo dough
12 tablespoons (6 ounces) unsalted butter, melted
2/3 cup finely ground almonds
Mint sprigs, for garnish

To prepare the filling, in a large sauté pan, place the pears, dates, orange juice, cinnamon, eau-de-vie, water and pepper. Cook over high heat 2 minutes, stirring constantly. Reduce the heat to medium and cook 10 to 12 minutes, stirring occasionally, until the mixture is thick. Remove from the heat, let cool to room temperature and transfer to a small bowl.

Preheat the oven to 375 F.

To assemble the rolls, lay 1 sheet of phyllo lengthwise on a flat surface. Keep the remaining sheets covered with a damp towel as you work. Using a pastry brush, lightly brush the single sheet of phyllo with melted butter. Sprinkle approximately 1 tablespoon of the ground almonds over the surface of the buttered phyllo. Cover with a second sheet of phyllo, lightly brush with butter and sprinkle with the nuts. Repeat layering using a third sheet of phyllo, butter and almonds. Top with a fourth sheet. Brush the top sheet with melted butter and omit the nuts.

Using approximately 6 rounded tablespoons of filling, spread the filling lengthwise

in a straight line across the phyllo 1 inch from the edge, leaving a 1-inch border on the sides. Roll the phyllo around the filling, tucking in the sides as you go to make a tight, fully enclosed roll. Place on a lightly greased baking sheet and lightly brush with melted butter. Make two more rolls using the same technique.

Bake the rolls 15 minutes on the bottom shelf of the oven. Rotate to the upper shelf and bake 5 to 7 minutes longer, or until the rolls are light golden brown. (Watch carefully; overbaking can result in leakage.) Remove from the oven and let stand at room temperature for 10 minutes. Cut into 2- or 3-inch slices. Garnish each serving with a sprig of mint and serve immediately. *Serves 8 to 10*

*Note:* Once baked and cooled, the rolls can be tightly wrapped in 2 layers of foil and frozen for up to 2 months. To reheat, place the foil-wrapped rolls in a medium oven until warmed through, approximately 10 minutes; remove the foil and bake an additional 3 minutes to crisp the phyllo.

# Caramelized Pear Galette

*Inspired by the classic French apple tart, this delicious pastry utilizes firm, nutty-tasting Bosc pears that are lightly cooked in a butter-sugar mixture before being added to the tart shell. It may be a little messy arranging the warm pears in the shell, but the rich, thick, caramelized glaze is well worth a few sticky fingers.*

**Crust:**
1/2 cup finely ground almonds
1 1/2 cups all-purpose flour
3 tablespoons granulated sugar
6 tablespoons chilled unsalted butter, cut into
    small pieces
2 tablespoons chilled solid vegetable shortening, cut
    into small pieces
1 to 1 1/2 tablespoons ice water

**Filling:**
4 tablespoons (1/2 stick) unsalted butter
3 firm Bosc pears, halved, cored and sliced lengthwise
    into 1/8-inch-thick wedges
1/2 cup tightly packed light brown sugar

Juice from 1 lemon

Lightly grease a 9-inch tart pan with a removable bottom.

To make the crust, in a large bowl, thoroughly combine the nuts, flour and sugar. Add the butter and the shortening. Working quickly, using brisk, rapid movements with your fingers, combine the butter and shortening with the dry ingredients until the mixture resembles coarse meal. Add just enough of the ice water to form the mixture into a cohesive ball.

Form the dough into a disc approximately 3 inches in diameter. Place in the center of the prepared tart pan. Using your fingers, gently push the dough across the bottom of the pan and up the sides, approximately 1/4 inch above the top edge of the pan. Pat the dough, making an even layer on the bottom and sides. To allow for shrinkage, using your thumb and forefinger, gently squeeze the extended dough into a tight 1/4-inch ridge above the rim and even with the interior sides. Cover with plastic wrap and refrigerate for 2 hours or up to 1 day.

Preheat the oven to 400 degrees F.

Prick the dough with a fork and line the pastry shell with parchment paper or foil. Add pie weights, dried beans or rice. Bake on the lower shelf of the oven 10 minutes. Remove pie weights and liner and bake 10 minutes longer, or until very light golden brown. Remove from the oven and let cool to room temperature before filling.

To make the filling, in a very large, nonstick sauté pan, melt the butter over medium-high heat, stirring often. Add the pears and cook 3

minutes, gently shaking the pan frequently to promote even cooking. Add the sugar and cook 3 minutes, or until the sugar has completely dissolved, stirring very carefully so as not to break the pears. Remove from the heat and let cool slightly.

Using a slotted spoon or your hands, carefully remove the pear slices from the liquid, taking care not to break them; reserve the butter-sugar mixture. Placing the short, rounded ends of the sliced pears against the outside edge of the pastry shell and the pointed (neck) ends toward the center, neatly arrange the pears in a concentric pattern, overlapping approximately 1/8 inch.

Cook the remaining butter-sugar mixture over high heat, stirring frequently, until it turns dark brown in color and is reduced to a thick, fairly syrupy consistency, approximately 5 minutes. Pour evenly over the pears.

Bake the filled tart shell on the top shelf of the oven for 25 to 30 minutes, or until the pears are tender and the liquid is very thick. Remove from the oven and drizzle with the lemon juice. Let cool to room temperature before slicing into wedges to serve. *Serves 6 to 8*

## Minted Pear Sorbet

*Serve this light and subtle pear-infused ice as a palate refresher between courses
or at the close of a rich meal with a glass of pear eau-de-vie, dessert wine or champagne.*

*1 cup water*
*1/4 cup fresh lemon juice*
*1/2 cup granulated sugar*
*2 cloves*

*3 ripe pears (preferably Comice, Bartlett or Red
Crimson), peeled, cored and coarsely chopped*
*2 teaspoons minced fresh mint leaves*
*Fresh mint sprigs, for garnish*

In a medium, heavy-bottomed saucepan, bring the water, lemon juice, sugar and cloves to a boil over high heat. Cook 10 to 12 minutes, stirring frequently to prevent the mixture from boiling over, until thick and syrupy and the liquid has reduced to approximately 1/2 cup. Add the pears, reduce the heat to medium-high and cook 8 to 10 minutes, stirring frequently, until the pears are tender and aromatic. Remove from the heat and let cool to room temperature.

Place the mixture in a blender along with the minced mint. Purée until smooth, stopping occasionally to scrape the sides of the container. Transfer to a nonreactive container, cover tightly and freeze at least 8 hours or up to 5 days. Remove from the freezer 5 to 10 minutes before serving. Mix vigorously and spoon into small, attractive glasses or tiny bowls. Serve immediately, garnished with mint sprigs.
*Serves 4 to 6*

## Pear Liqueur

*How does the whole pear get inside the narrow-necked bottle of pear eau-de-vie or pear liqueur?*
*The answer is simple. Once the pear blossom turns into a tiny fruit, a bottle is carefully placed over the*
*fruit and the branch. It is then sealed and left on the tree until the pear reaches maturity.*
*The bottle containing the pear is then removed from the tree and filled with the liqueur ingredients.*
*If you don't have a pear tree growing in your backyard, you can still make a superior homemade version*
*of pear liqueur for one-third the price of commercial brands by following this recipe.*

*1 large ripe pear (preferably Bartlett, Packham or*
    *Red Crimson)*
*4 cups vodka*

*1 1/2 cups superfine sugar*
*1/4 cup pear eau-de-vie*

Using a sharp fork, pierce the pear all over, taking care not to tear the skin or flesh. Place in a wide-mouth glass jar with a tight-fitting lid. Add the vodka and cover tightly. Store, undisturbed, at room temperature for 1 month.

After 1 month remove the lid and add the sugar; mix gently. Replace the lid and store at room temperature for at least 3 months or up to 6 months.

Remove the lid, add the pear eau-de-vie and mix gently. The liqueur is now ready to drink. *Makes 4 cups*

# METRIC CONVERSIONS

## Liquid Weights

| U.S. Measurements | Metric Equivalents |
|---|---|
| 1/4 teaspoon | 1.23 ml |
| 1/2 teaspoon | 2.5 ml |
| 3/4 teaspoon | 3.7 ml |
| 1 teaspoon | 5 ml |
| 1 dessertspoon | 10 ml |
| 1 tablespoon (3 teaspoons) | 15 ml |
| 2 tablespoons (1 ounce) | 30 ml |
| 1/4 cup | 60 ml |
| 1/3 cup | 80 ml |
| 1/2 cup | 120 ml |
| 2/3 cup | 160 ml |
| 3/4 cup | 180 ml |
| 1 cup (8 ounces) | 240 ml |
| 2 cups (1 pint) | 480 ml |
| 3 cups | 720 ml |
| 4 cups (1 quart) | 1 litre |
| 4 quarts (1 gallon) | 3 3/4 litres |

## Dry Weights

| U.S. Measurements | Metric Equivalents |
|---|---|
| 1/4 ounce | 7 grams |
| 1/3 ounce | 10 grams |
| 1/2 ounce | 14 grams |
| 1 ounce | 28 grams |
| 1 1/2 ounces | 42 grams |
| 1 3/4 ounces | 50 grams |
| 2 ounces | 57 grams |
| 3 ounces | 85 grams |
| 3 1/2 ounces | 100 grams |
| 4 ounces (1/4 pound) | 114 grams |
| 6 ounces | 170 grams |
| 8 ounces (1/2 pound) | 227 grams |
| 9 ounces | 250 grams |
| 16 ounces (1 pound) | 464 grams |

## Temperatures

| Fahrenheit | Celsius (Centigrade) |
|---|---|
| 32°F (water freezes) | 0°C |
| 200°F | 95°C |
| 212°F (water boils) | 100°C |
| 250°F | 120°C |
| 275°F | 135°C |
| 300°F (slow oven) | 150°C |
| 325°F | 160°C |
| 350°F (moderate oven) | 175°C |
| 375°F | 190°C |
| 400°F (hot oven) | 205°C |
| 425°F | 220°C |
| 450°F (very hot oven) | 230°C |
| 475°F | 245°C |
| 500°F (extremely hot oven) | 260°C |

## Length

| U.S. Measurements | Metric Equivalents |
|---|---|
| 1/8 inch | 3 mm |
| 1/4 inch | 6 mm |
| 3/8 inch | 1 cm |
| 1/2 inch | 1.2 cm |
| 3/4 inch | 2 cm |
| 1 inch | 2.5 cm |
| 1 1/4 inches | 3.1 cm |
| 1 1/2 inches | 3.7 cm |
| 2 inches | 5 cm |
| 3 inches | 7.5 cm |
| 4 inches | 10 cm |
| 5 inches | 12.5 cm |

## Approximate Equivalents

1 kilo is slightly more than 2 pounds
1 litre is slightly more than 1 quart
1 meter is slightly over 3 feet
1 centimeter is approximately 3/8 inch

# INDEX